MODERN CALLIGRAPHY IN FOUR EASY STEPS

The ART of Lettering

STEFAN KUNZ

HarperCollins*Publishers*

HarperCollins*Publishers*
1 London Bridge Street
London SE1 9GF
www.harpercollins.co.uk

First published by HarperCollins*Publishers* in 2017

Text by Kate Latham

A catalogue record for this book is available from
the British Library

ISBN 978-0-00-796626-4

Printed and bound in China

CONTENTS

INTRODUCTION

I taught myself lettering, so I want you to feel confident and happy to pick up a pencil, pen, or chalk and letter what you want to when you want to.

I hope that this book is a creative prompt and an encouragement to experiment and create projects and artworks that inspire you.

I often get asked how long I've been lettering and it is a very long time. As a kid, other than Lego, I only needed a pencil and some paper to keep me happy. I've been drawing since I was small. When I got older, I started designing quotes on my iPhone, and I realized that actually it would be easier to draw my own. I looked around me every day for inspiration and copied a lot until I learned how to write in the same style. From that came my own techniques and personal style. And it really was that easy. I love that I don't need complicated tools or expensive papers to create something meaningful, and I love that everything from the shape on the top of my frothy latte to my favorite artist or the writing on someone's shirt gives me new ideas.

What really helped me was remembering that it's only fun if you enjoy the learning—don't spend hours trying to create perfection. Lettering is about making something personal and individual; so have passion in what you create and be inspired.

So, let's go!

THE FOUR-STEP PROCESS

In learning the art of lettering, I came up with a four-step process that made me the confident student of the craft that I am now. And it's very simple to follow:

1. INSPIRATION

Most importantly, find the inspiration around you for letterforms. Look online at Instagram and Pinterest for lettering and artists that you love. Take photos of signs and typography that appeal to you, and find your inspiration.

2. COPY

Once you've found something that you love, then copy it. Over and over again. It is in the observing and copying that we learn how to letter and how to create. Don't worry about mistakes—lettering is individual and imperfect, just keep copying and practicing to find your style.

3. LEARN

Work your way through the techniques and letterforms in this book, then experiment with different strokes, shapes, and media. Once you understand the anatomy of the alphabet, you have the basic skills to move to the next step.

4. CREATE

Practice and knowledge allow you to develop your own alphabets and styles and become a lettering expert. So, have fun and get creating!

GETTING

Started

THE ESSENTIALS

Remember that lettering tools are largely a matter of personal choice. Find a good art store and experiment with the different media and paper you find there. It's always wise to invest in good-quality tools where you can. Here are some things you will need.

PENCILS AND ERASER

Pencils are either "H" (hard) or "B" (soft)—a higher number will give you a harder or softer lead for each type. I suggest starting with a 2H–4H for general shaping. B pencils are great if you want to use shading or lines that respond better to pressure and to create depth.

PENS AND INK

There is a world of nibbed pens and "edged" pens (pens with nibs or tips that offer different shapes for lettering) to explore. Use a pointed nib for simple lettering forms and an edged nib to give you letters with variations of width and shape. You could also try "automatic pens," which offer more extreme shapes for letter creation and design. Calligraphy pens have a reservoir for ink at the front or back of the pen base which can be loaded with ink or paint. Fiber-tip pens offer a more simple approach.

CHALKS

This is one time when you can get started with standard white school chalk—though anti-dust chalk gives a cleaner result.

COLORED PENCILS

These can be used for colored letters and lines, or for adding details and highlights.

PAINT

Watercolors and gouache are the best paints for lettering—you can use them with a quality sable brush or with most nib pens.

PAPER/CARD

Your choice of paper or card will depend on the finish you are looking for. Find a good art store and trial varying weights, textures, and colors. A good place to start is a basic "hot-pressed" (HP) paper, which is smoother than a watercolor paper (described as "not" hot-pressed) and less porous. A standard weight paper for lettering is 140lb index or 140lb cover (or around 250gsm).

RULER, SET SQUARE, AND FRENCH CURVE

These are invaluable to create smooth and precise lines and curves.

SCALPEL, CUTTING BOARD, AND ADHESIVE

You will need a good quality scalpel or utility knife (and spare blades) plus a cutting mat, and quality waterproof adhesive/PVA.

You may also find it helpful and useful to have the following to hand: paper towels for spills and smudges, scrap paper to protect your work when you are in the process, masking tape to secure your paper to a solid surface, and tracing paper to help you copy and correct letterforms within your design.

THE BASICS

Choose a simple pencil, pen, or chalk that you are comfortable with and let's get started.

First, rule yourself some lines, or invest in calligraphy lined paper, and start practicing some lettering strokes.

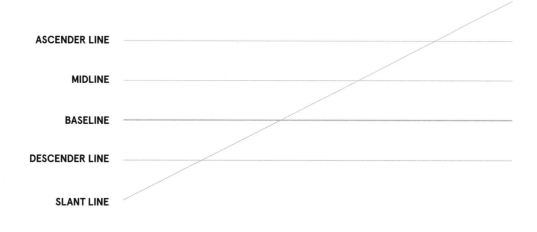

ASCENDER LINE

MIDLINE

BASELINE

DESCENDER LINE

SLANT LINE

FORMING STROKES

Try downward strokes first—keeping the pen nib in line with the angle of the stroke. Begin with an upright line, then try at an angle. Push the pen firmly downward, before lifting cleanly from the paper.

Form upward strokes next—pulling the pen smoothly and lightly.

Now try a curved stroke—like an "n" shape. Move lightly up the shape and apply more pressure coming back down.

Finally, practice a rounded shape, draw a "c" shape with your pen, then trace an "o" shape. Keep the letter upright to the vertical axis at first, then try repeating the letter on a slant.

MAKING LETTERS

Quite simply, lines plus curves make shapes. Shapes make letters. So, don't be scared and get lettering.

It's easiest to practice groups of similar letters together. Pick a group, set up your guidelines and then try out the letters to a vertical axis. Then adjust the angle of your letters to a chosen slant line and try each set again.

a   e   o   c

h   b   d   l

g   j   q   p   y

u   w   m   n

Watch the weight of each stroke and try to ensure that each letter is consistent.

Now, take one letter from each group and repeat it over and over, keeping the strokes aligned and identical in pressure and spacing.

Once you have practiced your basic lettering shapes, it's time to try the real thing!

a

b

g

w

SANS SERIF

SERIF

SANS SERIF

Now, it's time to take on your first alphabet. Sans serif letters, also known as gothic, are basic clean letterforms, perfect for starting out. Dominant and modern in style, they are easy to distinguish as they are "sans" (without) any extension or "foot" at the beginnings and ends of the letters. Sans serif typefaces that you might recognize are Helvetica, Futura, and Franklin Gothic.

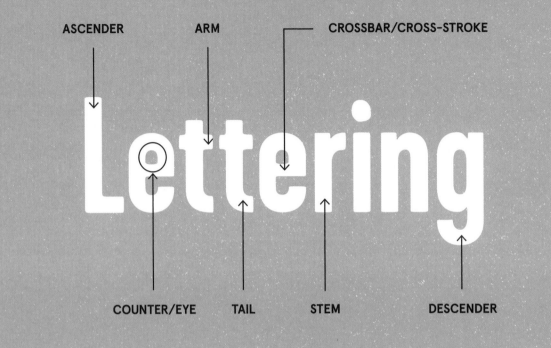

ASCENDER   ARM   CROSSBAR/CROSS-STROKE

COUNTER/EYE   TAIL   STEM   DESCENDER

To get started, trace over the gray sans serif word below.

Lettering

Now, using the medium with which you feel most comfortable, begin copying the letters here, and practicing. Once you have the feel of the letter shapes, find some examples of sans serif alphabets you would like to develop further.

This is the most basic letterform from which all your lettering will stem. Play around with the height of the ascenders and descenders, the angle of the letters, and the width of the characters to change the style of your alphabet.

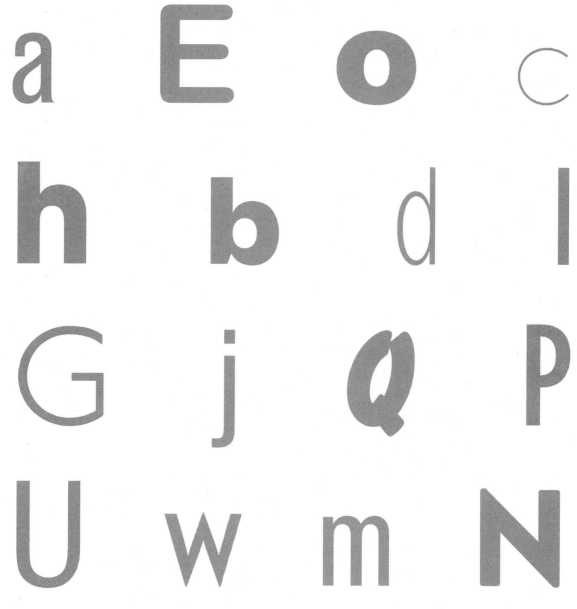

Use these pages to practice what you have learned.

SERIF

a e o c
h b d l
g j q p
u w m n

SERIF

The serif or roman style of typography is characterized by the "foot" at the beginning or end of the letter. This style originated with the Latin alphabet, and was developed as an inscriptional lettering style. It is generally used for body text as it's easier for the eye to read than a sans serif alphabet. It's also a great style to make your own.

Look at the serif fonts you see all around you and you'll soon see the wonderful variations of styles and the impact they create.

Typography

SERIF/FOOT   LOOP   BRACKET

Practice some serif letters by overworking the word below.

Typography

Now, take a clean piece of paper and start practicing your serif lettering. Play with different types of "serif"—hairline and thick, straight and curved. And experiment with different angles within your letters: move your crossbars higher and lower on the letters or draw them on a slant, make your counters round or square, and add exaggeration to the curve of the stems.

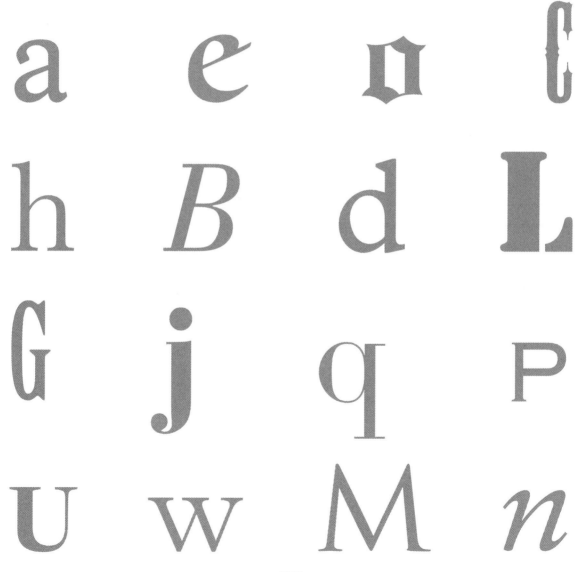

Now try lettering the name of your favorite
book, film, or person. How do they differ, and
what style works best for each?

Try an italic style of lettering—serif to a slanted
line—for a more personal style of writing.

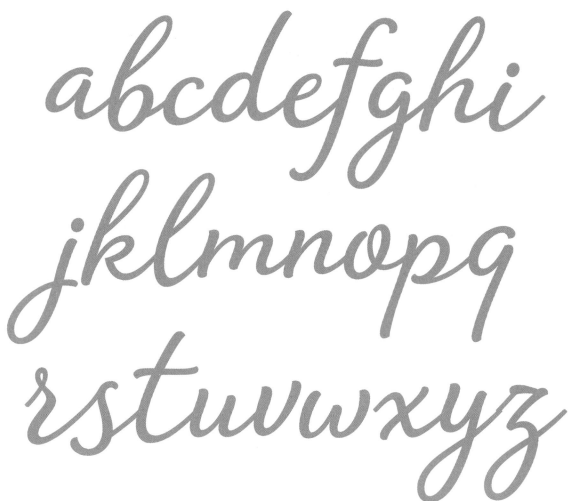

SCRIPT

At first, script may look more complicated, but it's just using a flowing form to create a styled alphabet that resembles handwriting. Similar to the italic style you've just been trying, script is more of a free-form lettering style and wonderful for adding warmth to your lettering projects.

Beautiful

The best way to copy a script is to observe slant, letter thickness, and the added details at the beginnings and ends of words. Joining letters together can be done simply or by adding loops or flourishes. Practice here by writing over the letterforms of this word.

This style also lends itself to a greater movement and shape in the word—don't feel pressured to stick to the baseline or midline, just let the letters flow.

Once you have practiced some basic script styles, try creating your own. You don't have to create a complete alphabet, just try drawing a handful of common letters to the same style.

Then take a look and decide if letters look like they belong together. Look at the shapes, the spaces around the letters, and the flourishes you have used to add character. It won't be perfect, but learn from what does and doesn't work for next time. Practice with groups of words until you are writing confidently.

Now you are ready to start bringing your lettering styles together.

COMBINING

lettering

Now that you have mastered basic lettering, you can start
to put together words to make bigger artwork. Bringing
together different styles is part of the fun of lettering—there
are few rules, it's about how you choose to express yourself.
Here are some tips for this next stage.

BLOCKING

To start a piece like this, begin by deciding what words or letters you are going to use, and "block" out the text areas in pencil to build your grid.

GRID SHAPES AND BASELINES

It is probably easiest to begin with grids made from simple shapes and straight lines. Once you're confident with these, then play around with shapes, angles, and baselines.

EMPHASIS

Once you have your layout sorted, it's really helpful to decide where you want the emphasis of your piece to be. Just as we use capitals and italics to draw out certain words and phrases when we are typing, in lettering we use different styles and types of letters to bring focus to a piece. Deciding this at the beginning of your project will ensure that your design has the impact that you want.

SPACING

Spacing your work correctly is important. "Kerning" is the spacing between letters on a line, and "leading" is the spacing between the lines of text. Creating an even piece of lettering isn't as simple as using equal measurements between letters and lines, you'll need to use your eyes to adjust the kerning and leading to create a visual sense of equal space—allowing more or less space than the standard for certain combinations of letters to avoid words appearing squashed or choppy on the page.

Spacing

Spacing

Ascenders and descenders affect how much
leading you need for each artwork also, so bear
this in mind when working out your grid.

Watch out for difficult letters and lettering combinations, and as you work, keep stopping to look at your piece and check the spacing.

And also experiment with the spacing between words on the same line—too much space can make the piece look strange, too little and you risk the reader struggling to make sense of your words.

DIVIDERS

Sometimes, to add shape or "punctuation" to your piece, you may want to use a divider or separating feature to ease legibility or sense. Everything from small dots and lines to a small border can help you add shape and meaning within a piece.

GRAMMAR AND PUNCTUATION

And speaking of punctuation, do remember to check your spelling and punctuation before you start inking. I learned this rule the hard way!

Practice combining your lettering below.

BANNERS

Now you're confident about your lettering skills, try new ways of displaying your letters. Banners can be big or small, formal or fun. In fact, it's just lettering within a shape. The facing page shows a selection of different banner styles.

DRAWING A SIMPLE BANNER

To create a simple banner, think of your wording before you decide on a shape. Make sure your choice is the correct size and will suit the style of your lettering.

To draw the banner, start with the biggest part or centerpiece of the banner. Draw the two parallel lines, then join them together.

Next, add your tail- or endpieces on either side. Then pencil in the joining piece/fold between.

Once you're happy with the outline, then add the lettering within it. Remember that the baseline of your lettering will follow the shape of your banner. Check and check again before inking it all.

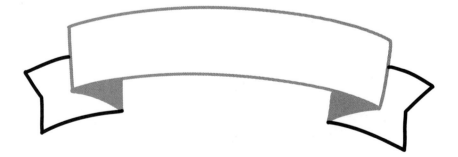

REVERSED-OUT LETTERING

A shaded or colored banner with reversed-out writing works in exactly the same way. Mark out your lettering carefully before inking around the letters rather than inside them.

SHADING AND SHADOWS

For banners in particular, shading adds an extra dimension to your art and adds to the 3-D sense of the piece. To work out how to shadow your letters or shapes, first decide where your light source is in motion to the banner—from which point all your shadows will be formed.

Think of capital letters as a great opportunity to have fun with your projects. Whether you're SHOUTING your words or merely punctuating with capital letters, they are a wonderfully fun addition to your lettering experiments.

CAPITAL LETTERS

With capital letters, it is even more important to remember the purpose and style of your artwork when you style them, as they drive the feel of your piece adding drama or fun to your lettering.

ORNATE/ORNAMENTAL CAPITALS

By way of adding detail to your work without over-garnishing the entire piece, creating a highly embellished capital is a quick means to decorate your art. Add lots of flourishes for a filigree letter, or try a gothic style to add a sense of occasion.

INFILLED/PATTERNED CAPITALS

We've talked about the shape of the letter, but don't just consider the outside, think about how you can fill the letter. Whether shading, adding inlay patterns or flowers, or a geometric style, have fun with the space inside the lines on these letters.

DROPPED CAPITALS

From the times of illuminated manuscripts, drop caps were common to initiate the openings of chapters and quotes. As per the name, they tend to extend below the baseline of the rest of the text, and often also above the ascender line to make a statement. Embellish them or add patterns inside as you wish.

FREESTYLE

Without worrying about creating an entire alphabet in a style—practice a range of capital letters in different styles. Be big and bold in your lettering.

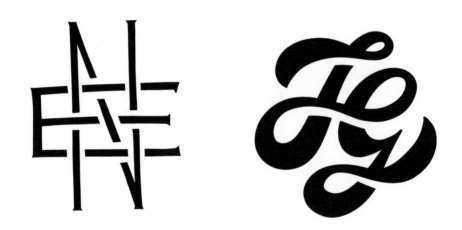

MONOGRAMS

A monogram is a name represented by two or more capital letters joined together.

Experiment with different styles to create a monogram for yourself or a friend.

BORDERS

Just as capital letters and banners add movement and decoration to your lettering, borders and frames give definition and bring a piece together visually. You can choose simple, rigid designs for a "hard" border or more flowing, looser styles to create a "free" border. Similarly, don't feel that borders need to be defined rectangle or circle shapes—try freestyle borders without a fixed shape.

If your border has corners or angles where straight lines meet, see these as opportunities to introduce new design elements for extra impact—a curvy flourish on a hard line border or a small motif in the space where lines would meet can be much easier to draw, too!

Take a small piece of lettering, and repeat it with four different borders—try a small geometric pattern, a wavy leafy style, a simple line of dots, and a delicate scrollwork design. Look at the different impacts generated by the borders and how they visually change the wording inside.

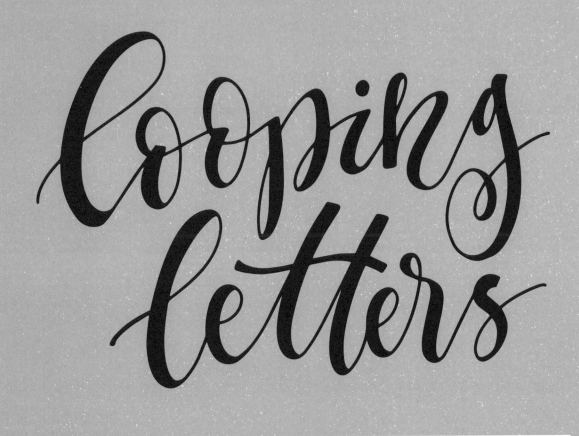

Looping letters

As your designs become more complex and refined, be brave with your lettering styles. Here, a simple script style is developed into exaggerated looping letters, often called "brush lettering," as the effect given is painted rather than created with a simple nib shape. This effect comes from a greater use of thick and fine lines on your lettering with added loops to form the letters. It's a beautiful style for hand-lettering projects with a very personal and traditional feel.

To start with, take three letters— try l, a, and h—and practice them over and over. Play around with the loops on the letters—make them bigger and smaller and watch how the letter changes.

Apply more pressure on the down strokes and less as your pen moves upward. Keep your hand relaxed as you letter and enjoy creating—this style is less about following the lines and more about keeping your shapes flowing. Work with your own handwritting to create your own personal style of looping letters, as shown in the three variations below.

Once you have experimented with your basic letters, try different letters—those with ascenders and descenders offer great potential for looping fun. Then try a handful of capital letters—and use open loop shapes to give a more freehand shape to your words.

As you play around with looping letters, you'll find that place where embellishment is maximized without compromising on legibility. Remember, your words must still be legible—watching that your letters are uniform is a good way of ensuring that the reader "understands" and can read your lettering style.

THE 30-DAY CHALLENGE

When I first started lettering, I decided to challenge myself to practice for at least ten minutes every day for 30 days. Practice, practice, and more practice is the best way to learn how to letter, and the most rewarding. Choose small projects to give you that feeling of accomplishment quickly—it will help you keep your challenge going. Why not decide to make ten hand-lettered thank you notes for friends and family? Or write special name cards for a family celebration?

INSPIRATION

And finally, as an end to this section on tips and tricks to take your lettering skills further, think back to my Four-Step Process to learning how to letter:

1. INSPIRATION
2. COPY
3. LEARN
4. CREATE

Before you can create, take lots of time to copy and learn. Practice, practice, and more practice will give you the skills and confidence to do great things and make great projects with your lettering talent. And most of all, have fun with it.

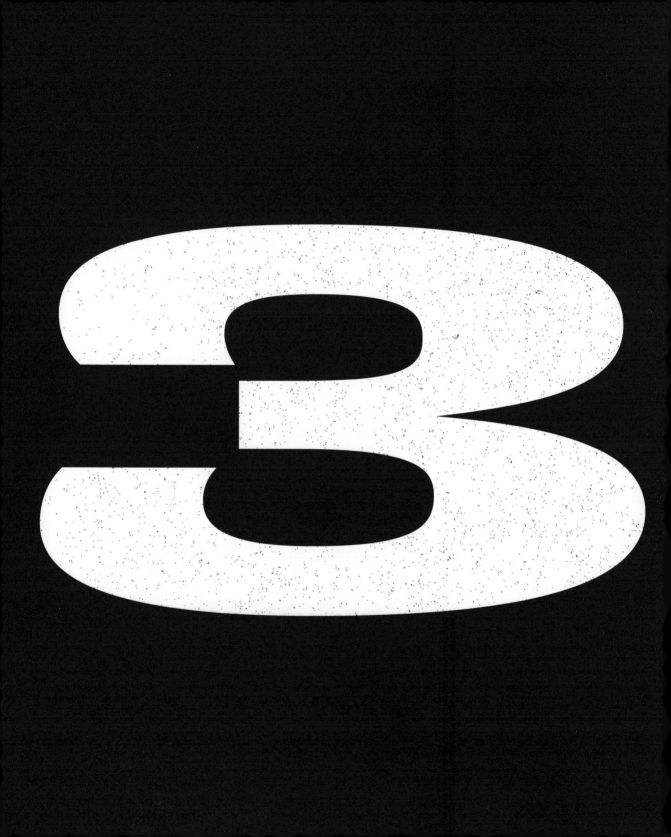

Copy the different letter styles here to practice your lettering.

Once you're confident with your letter styles, try different shapes and sizes for each word or group of words to get your message across.

Build up your letters slowly to create new styles—I often end up
with something completely different to what I intended.

Mix and match your scripts, styles, embellished lettering, and flourishes—and
remember, you can always erase something if it's not working.

Try capitals for clear, dynamic lettering and quotes—and you
can still bring in different styles to add simple drama.

For negative space lettering, sketch out your letters within the border,
banner, or shape carefully before filling in around them.

When you're combining different scripts, practice them
separately first before you start a full piece.

Choose a single word or phrase as your creative spark for a project.

Sometimes using a single writing style can create the most effective design.

If you're using one design style, take the time to balance out the shape of the quote, keep your lines smooth and flowing, and add flourishes sparingly.

Remember to have fun with your lettering practice—add flourishes, swashes, swirls, and details to create the mood.

Practice a quote that means something to you—be passionate about your lettering.

Now you should feel more confident about breaking the rules and bringing together different styles for impact.

Think about where your quote might feature and who will see it when you decide what style to create.

Feel free to push your lettering boundaries.
Play creatively and try out tricky fonts.

Let shadows and shapes be part of the writing too.

Using banners and borders in your writing helps give shape and depth to your words, and provides a useful grounding to the quote.

Shading, stippling, and gradiated letters can bring together heavy types with lighter, handwritten, or cursive letterforms.

I'm most proud when something comes together after careful planning. This isn't perfect, but I like the shape, playfulness, and lines of the letterforms.

Using contrasting lettering styles with similar decorations and details allows different types to work alongside each other.

Impact is everything—if it's not working, don't be afraid to stop and start again. But save your first attempt—it's likely that you'll use it again somehow.

Doodle as much as you can—letting your pen or pencil make shapes and play with strokes is the best way to improve your technique and develop your own style.

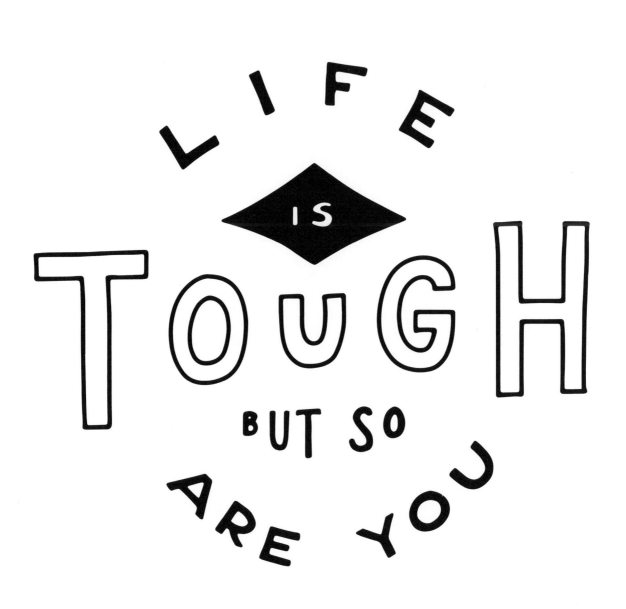

LIFE IS TOUGH BUT SO ARE YOU

Sometimes the simplest designs can be the strongest—use
your skills sparingly to allow the message to shout!

It's most important on simple designs to be careful about your spacing—your kerning and
leading. If you're not sure—turn your page upside down for a clearer sense of space.

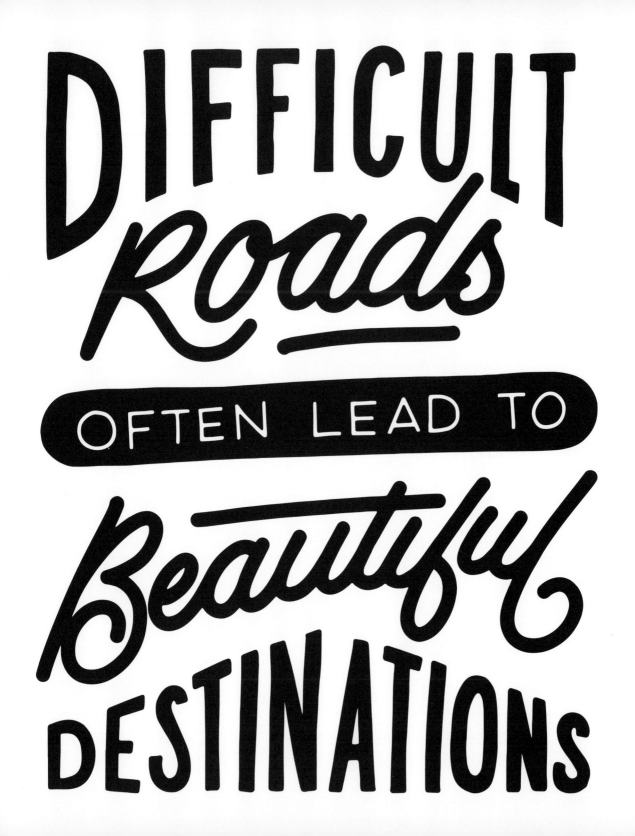

Cursive and script writing makes your words seem warm and inviting,
and can be easier to create and more forgiving in the design!

Practicing your signature is a great way of trying out different styles.
Try bold, antique, fun, and crazy styles for your name.

Combinations of flourishes, ligatures, and complicated serifs
take time to bring together. Practice, plan, and enjoy!

Build up your own "library" of font ideas: snippets from magazines,
photographs of signs that you like the look of, and ideas that spark joy.

These days, we use emoticons to show what we're feeling with our typed messages—hand lettering allows us to express exactly what we want to say through our choice of design.

Break any lettering rules you want to—keep practicing and playing and you can look forward to making your mark in a more permanent fashion.

This is the first "shout out" about your wedding and the first visual indication of your wedding "style." If you can, choose an alphabet, a lettering style, and/or a mood that you will follow throughout your wedding stationery and decor.

You are
CORDIALLY
INVITED
TO THE
Wedding
OF
Amanda
— & —
BRANDON

OCTOBER 27 TH
5:00 IN THE AFTERNOON
HILTON HOTEL

This example is a modern announcement. Remember that the invitation holds a huge amount of crucial information—legibility trumps style on this one! Find a printer who can suggest the printing options, card stock, and colors with you, and always look at samples before printing.

Having stand-out on your RSVP card makes it more likely that your guests will remember to reply in time! By now, your wedding theme and colors are more likely to be confirmed, so use this card to bring in elements of your special day.

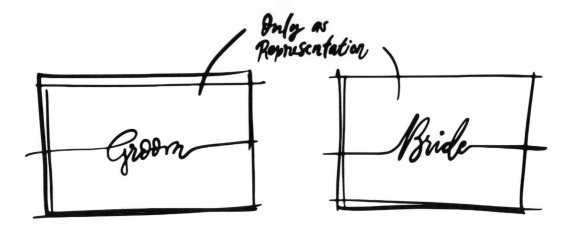

Only as Representation

Groom

Bride

Bride

Groom

Marie

These small cards are a wonderful touch for the wedding breakfast tables, and a great personal project. Give yourself plenty of time to complete them, and keep in mind how they are going to be presented on the tables. Don't be afraid to use colored inks or backgrounds.

The final lettering project of your wedding and arguably the most important. This represents what your wedding meant to you and is a lasting reminder for your guests of the event, so don't hold back!

Deck
THE · HALLS
with
BOUGHS
OF
Holly

A simple card design is often the best place to begin your official lettering project work. Take the time to plan your layout and experiment with different media, colors, and styles for a wonderful handcrafted greeting.

Whether formal, decorative, funny, or tongue-in-cheek—allow your lettering to flow and your decorations to set off your type. This would make a wonderful wall hanging as well as a card. Alternatively, work the design onto chalkboard or glass, or even in chalk on your front path for a very seasonal effect.

A simple gift card is a lovely detail to handcraft. Here, Christmas "ribbons" of lettering make a great representational style, and shading/shadowing gives a wonderful 3-D effect.

And for a completely different feel to your seasonal message, play around with retro or script fonts to invoke a specific era. These would make fantastic cards as well as tags or Christmas artworks. Again, experiment with types of media, colors, and backgrounds to suit the recipient.

Again, use the playfulness of the fonts and have fun with the "line" of the type to give a more fun and modern feel. It can take a while to get the balance right, so experiment before you get out the good card.

I love using strong types to make simple dramatic statements. In our day of mass-produced pictorial cards, a simple design on a heavy-weight card makes a huge statement. And for fun, choose a dayglow color background or random pattern to have fun with this design.

Here, a simple style followed throughout the lettering gives a beautiful sense of occasion.
Remember with decorative fonts that legibility is more important than ornament.

This acrostic-style design just cries out to sample some freestyle letterforms. It would make a fantastic card, but don't stop there: why not make a larger artwork for framing?

Here, a heavy cursive font combines drama and warmth. Use this stark design against a simple plain background or set off against color or pattern for more fun.

Play around with some new fonts you've created, using whatever words you can bring into the design. Note how the type styles here complement the characteristic featured and present a striking visual.

Celebrating a new arrival is a very special occasion, so create a unique congratulations to mark the event. This project allows you to letter a special card or artwork to give—something that will be treasured always.

In this project, see how the choice of alphabet or font changes the mood of the piece, making it softer with a more romantic style. Play around with funny or classic alphabets or reversed-out lettering for a different effect. Here too, I've chosen a banner style that allows flexibility for the lengths of your chosen wording.

This would look fantastic framed on a nursery wall. I used lettering styles that contrast and complement each other—with lots of flourishes to mirror the script. You could just as easily add a border of baby motifs or the baby's name and birth details for a different surround.

Remember to use color to bring your artwork to life, whether it's within the letters, banners, reversed out lettering, or patterns within the letters. Using strong or muted colors can give a very different vibe to this project.

Often the best designs are the simplest. Remember to think about where and how your project will be displayed or used, as well as its recipient, when you are practicing and sketching it out.

A fun project and a great way to liven up your kitchen, or as a gift for a friend's new home. Play around with the script to complement the kitchen, and create something to make you dance!

I love this as a striking piece for an entryway or hall. Use a lettering style that works with your decor or house style. It would also work brilliantly as a chalkboard/chalk wall project.

This piece is a great example of lettering styles reflecting mood and volume! Just as capital letters make our typed words "shout," here a dramatic visual lettering style brings drama and fun to a design.

Yum! In this artwork, you can almost smell the coffee! Deceptively simple, I used perspective carefully on the lettering for a 3-D effect. Look at signage everywhere you go, plus pictures on Instagram and Pinterest, to learn how to give your alphabets this sense of depth.

Now you're confident in your lettering skills, have fun with words and illustrations together. Here's a chance to dunk your favorite quote into a more visual form. Now, where are the cookies?

This would be a perfect gift for someone who really knows how to cook up a storm. Choose your outline shape to match the theme of your project, start simple, but then you can ink into the shape of anything.

I love the "Stay Calm ... " quotes that are everywhere so this was my chance to use that format for my own slogan. This would also look great inked onto a plain mug with ceramic pens.

This looks complicated, but was so much fun to design. Break up your space into sections and shapes and see how many styles you can work together. Here, the larger lettering is the most fun, but the key to the whole piece working is the careful placement and design of the smaller words. You rock!

Simple, strong lettering projects like this are great for practice as you need to be precise when the lettering is so sparse. Look at examples to get a greater sense of how to use spacing to help you, and remember to trust your instincts about what you know will work. Lettering is 95 percent practice and 5 percent instinct.

And in contrast, this ornate lettering project has a completely different feel. Practice with a variety of media for different styles of work: ink is great for flowing shapes, and chalks and pencils for shading.

There is nothing more meaningful than a handcrafted thank you note, and if you design your project carefully, you could make it into a template on card or plastic so that it is much quicker to repeat next time.

Surprise your favorite teacher with this modern, fluid design, and take the freedom
to freestyle as you like or use illustrations and motifs personal to them.

Here, I have combined background shapes, banners, and textures for a striking piece for the one you love, a beautiful and creative antidote to the mass-produced cards that everyone else gives and receives.